Get Your First LNC Case: An Easy-to-Follow Guide for LNC Success

Pat Iyer MSN RN LNCC

Get Your First LNC Case

Copyright © 2022 Pat Iyer. All rights reserved. No part of this book can be reproduced in any form without the written permission of the author and its publisher.

The content in this book is for educational and informational purposes only. This material will support and assist readers in obtaining their goals, but ultimate success depends on their personal effort, motivation, commitment and follow through. The author cannot predict the reader's results and does not guarantee a particular result. Results differ for everyone, depending on their unique skills and efforts.

Publisher
The Pat Iyer Group
Fort Myers, FL

Table of Contents

Introduction 9

Chapter 1 Is Legal Nurse Consulting Right for You? 13

Chapter 2 What's Your House Worth? ... 15

Chapter 3 My First Case 19

Chapter 4 Lessons from the First and Subsequent Cases 23

Chapter 5 Risk Taking 27

Chapter 6 Overcoming Risks in Legal Nurse Consulting 33

Chapter 7 What Does it Take to Get Started? 39

Chapter 8 Paths to Getting Cases 43

Chapter 9 How One Client Became Many 61

Chapter 10 No Regrets............................. 65

Chapter 11 The First Step 69

Chapter 12 Getting Help 79

Other Books by Pat Iyer........................... 83

About the Author 93

Introduction

A successful legal nurse consultant has the satisfaction of being able to help his or her clients win their cases. And winning may mean different things depending upon who the nurse is working with. For a plaintiff attorney, winning the case means settling the case. If they can't settle the case, the plaintiff attorneys win by trying the case and getting an award from a jury.

For the defense attorney, it means settling a case for as small an award as possible, or if the case goes to trial, of getting a jury verdict in favor of the defense.

Being skilled at helping attorneys means that a legal nurse consultant has the satisfaction of helping clients win their cases. And it also means that the nurse has the potential to build up (if he or she wants) a full-time business helping attorneys.

Expert witnesses may not be full-time because they may be involved in their clinical or teaching roles. But nurses who help attorneys behind the scenes as consultants can build successful full-time businesses assisting attorneys.

After starting in the field as an expert witness in 1987, I began supplying experts in 1989 and formally established my business, Med League Support Services. I ran this business from 1987 until 2015, when I sold the company. After a six-year hiatus, I came back into legal nurse consulting in 2021.

Success meant that I created a business that employed four full-time staff. I had a 3600 square foot office. I used my business skills to build a very successful business that I could sell.

My company grossed more than a million dollars a year for the last five years I owned the company. Its income made it an attractive business for a buyer. I emphasize that I was able to sell because it's challenging to sell a service business, particularly one where the clients are attracted to the company because they feel comfortable and safe with its owner. They feel like they're in good hands with the person in charge.

Working with a business broker after trying to sell the company on my own ultimately resulted in me being able to sell the company and walk away and know that I had put it in good hands. The company is sustaining itself quite nicely today.

My company's success enables me to live part-time in New Jersey and part-time in Florida to avoid snow and ice, which is my big ambition. My husband grew up in India, and neither of us is interested in being in really cold, icy, rainy, sleety conditions any longer.

There's no need for me to go to an office. I can run my business out of my home.

I now help other legal nurse consultants build their businesses and achieve the level of success that satisfies them.

That's how my life turned out after mastering the challenges of being an entrepreneur.

Chapter 1 Is Legal Nurse Consulting Right for You?

Are you looking for a way to utilize your knowledge so that you don't have to continue in work that is increasingly more stressful and more physically and emotionally demanding?

Here's what I suspect is true about you.
- You believe there's something more you can do with that knowledge.
- You are intrigued by the detail-oriented aspects of this profession.
- You like solving puzzles; you like digging through medical records.
- You like figuring out what happened.
- You like the small precise bits of data that go into a report.
- You enjoy pulling information out of the medical records and utilizing your nursing knowledge to help attorneys.
- You want to employ your skills in a different way than when you're taking care of patients.

There are overlapping areas of skills between nursing and legal nurse consulting. When you spend time as a legal nurse consultant, you educate attorneys. When you spend time as a nurse, you educate patients and families.

Your communication skills are essential in both roles. The skills have different purposes when you're working with attorneys than when you're working with patients or you're communicating with colleagues, physicians, and other people in a medical environment.

The nurse is the bridge between the medical records and the attorney. The savvy attorney comes to value a nurse's perspective education and begins to wonder what they did without you.

Chapter 2 What's Your House Worth?

Although I shared with you that I was able to sell my successful LNC business, my life was not always that positive. In the 1980s, my husband and I were close to bankruptcy.

A year after I finished my master's degree in nursing, in 1980, we borrowed a million dollars to purchase a building in an urban area. My husband wanted to start a welding business and make parts for plastic extrusion machines. To get that money, we had to promise that everything we owned could be taken from us if we didn't satisfy the loans. This is a "personal guarantee," and it was the only condition under which we were able to borrow a million dollars.

After three years, that business failed due partly to some management issues, but the primary cause was the interest rate of 24% a month to pay back the borrowed money. And there wasn't any way that the company would ever make enough money to repay the loans.

In 1983, when I was pregnant with our second son, we risked losing everything we owned. I had visions of living on the street and having my children in a cardboard box next to me.

When I was six months pregnant, the man from the bank came through and looked at our house. My husband pointed out the water stain on the wall, the furnace that had problems, and all the other flaws so that the bank representative would not put a high number on it.

My husband negotiated with the people who lent us the money. If he repaid them 10 cents for every dollar that we borrowed, they agreed to forgive the rest of our debt. Due to his negotiation skills, we kept the house.

At that same time, my mother became anxious about the $10,000 she had personally loaned us to help us start the business. She wanted to make sure she would get her money back, so she asked my husband and me to give her the $10,000 back, which depleted our bank account.

I remember sitting in the hospital coffee shop (where I worked) with a friend. I had tears running down my face as I told her how vulnerable I felt. Why was my mother asking us for the money at this point when we had so little? However, she was worried about her own security because she was between her second and third husband, and she wasn't sure if she would ever see that money again.

We wrote her a check for the loan. You don't walk away from a loan that your mother gave you. We satisfied the lenders and then picked ourselves up and considered our next pathway.

I delivered my son and went back to work about two months after he was born. My nursing salary provided us with a solid safety net while my husband started a business in the living room of our house as a sales rep.

People have approached me frequently over the years to ask if I was interested in borrowing money for my business. And I always say, "No, if I don't have the money in the bank to pay for something, I don't want to take a loan." That personal guarantee experience and the near bankruptcy scarred both of us.

Chapter 3 My First Case

I became involved in legal nurse consulting as a direct result of going to a one-day program taught by a nurse who presented career alternatives for nurses. I had never heard about the idea of nurses working with attorneys. I had a vague knowledge that there were lawsuits. You can't practice nursing without knowing that patients sue healthcare providers, but I didn't understand how I could get involved in the legal field.

On the strength of having co-authored my first book in 1986, I acted on my interest in this new role of becoming an expert witness.

I went to the hospital attorney when I came out of that one-day program, and I said, "I'd like to become an expert witness; how do I get started?"

He explained how I could find a directory of attorneys who handled medical malpractice cases in my state and then look at a publication that described various jury verdicts and settlements. Putting these two pieces of information together, I determined which attorneys were handling medical malpractice cases so I could approach them.

I sat down, and I thought about it. Should I take this step? I had never done anything like this before. "I'm going to try," I told myself.

I sent out 20 letters to attorneys offering my services as a medical-surgical expert witness. Almost immediately, an attorney called me and said, "I've got a case, and I need a nursing expert. Would you review it for me?" Peter gave me that first opportunity to look at his case and assist him with the case as an expert witness.

Peter was defending a hospital where a young girl was suing the nurses. The plaintiff got out of bed around six o'clock in the morning. She had a fever. She didn't ask for help before she went into the bathroom and fainted. Her glass IV bottle shattered on the floor, resulting in her getting glass into her knee, leaving a significant scar. She blamed the nurses for her injury.

I looked at this case, and I said to the attorney, "I don't think the nurses did anything wrong. She didn't ask for help. They found her on the floor; they couldn't have known she was going to get up and get out of bed by herself."

When the attorney received my report, he called me and said, "Pat, this is not the right format for reports. You put footnotes in it and quoted from references. You have to do this over." He patiently took me through that process and showed me what I was supposed to be doing. I revised the report and sent it to him.

Next, the defense attorney called me up, laughing, and said the case was dismissed with prejudice. When the plaintiff's attorney got my report, he pulled out his checkbook and gave this young girl a check from his own law firm and said, "Look, they're not going to settle this case. We're not going to win it to go to trial. Take this money, and just leave."

After asking my client what dismissal with prejudice meant (the client took the money), I said, "Does that happen very often?" He said, "No, Pat, no, it doesn't happen very often. But it's over. You're done." Peter gave me cases for the next 25 years.

I continued to get calls from the attorneys who received letters and reviewed cases as a liability expert. I testified hundreds of times at deposition or trial and grew to enjoy the analytical nature of the role.

Chapter 4 Lessons from the First and Subsequent Cases

One of the most important lessons I learned through the experience of working as an expert witness was to be analytical. An expert must evaluate large amounts of data, prepare that material in a logical way, and, depending on the venue, write tightly constructed reports.

An expert uses communication skills in a new way. I have always enjoyed patient education. Educating attorneys was much like teaching patients.

That skill enabled me to move from being a clinical educator, which I started doing after completing my master's degree in nursing, to being self-employed. Within six months after the career alternatives for nursing seminar, I resigned from my job.

In addition to consulting and teaching, my expert witness work enabled me not to depend on an employer or to get mired in the politics that were part of being in nursing administration.

And also, being an entrepreneur enabled me to earn a living without having to drive on the highways every day. And I emphasize that because I drove an hour and 15 minutes, one way to my last job, which was in 1987 (the last time I got a paycheck from anyone), over heavily trafficked roads. At the end of the year, I was exhausted. I realized how much risk I was putting myself in by driving on that highway every day.

I wanted the autonomy of not being an employee and not being caught up in that heavy traffic.

Picture this. One summer day, while I was an employee, I decided I wanted to take the day off. It was a beautiful day, and the weather was predicted to be 80 degrees, clear, sunny. I wanted to take my sons to the beach. New Jersey has a beautiful coastline.

I called up my boss, and I said, "Something has come up. I need to have the day off tomorrow."

I took my kids to the beach. And the next day, when I went to work, my boss asked me very solicitously if my family emergency got resolved. I looked at her, and I thought, "Family emergency?" Without thinking, I said, "I didn't have a family emergency. I wanted to take my kids to the beach." She gave me a look of astonishment, glared at me, and walked away.

I thought I must have stunned her by telling her the truth. At that moment, I knew I did not want to ask anyone for permission to take my kids to the beach. Being self-employed enabled me to take the day off in the future when I wanted to.

Chapter 5 Risk Taking

You're sitting in your home thinking, "Do I want to get involved in this specialty field of nursing? Would I love to be able to take off a day without asking permission? What is it like to work with attorneys? How do I face the risks?"

By risks, I mean you're putting your foot out into new territory. You've gained a new skill set by going through some type of a legal nurse consulting program, whether it's online or in person, or self-paced, or in a college course. You're intrigued by this, but you're afraid that you won't be any good at it. You're worried that no one will hire you.

You fear that you could make mistakes and cost everybody a lot of time and money. You're wondering, "Is it worth the risk? Is it something that you should do?"

Perhaps you are surrounded by people who say, "Do you really want to do this? Attorneys are all sharks; they're all unethical. They'll just chew you up and spit you out.

Being in business is scary. What if you're no good at it? What if you screw up? The doubters in your life may tell you the things that you're worried about yourself.

And as you listen to those negative people, you say, "Do I really want to do this? Is this something that I should take the risk on? But if I don't take a risk, I will be walking the halls of the hospital or the nursing home or the same-day surgery unit forever."

Suppose you're a homecare nurse, case manager, or surveyor for a governmental agency. You're in the car, driving from place to place to place. You could be driving all over your state every day. You're working 10-to-12-hour shifts. Do you want to do that for your entire nursing career?

If you don't take the risk, how do you see your life? Will you end up with back injuries from lifting heavy people in bed? Will you stick yourself with dirty needles? Will a patient assault you?

Violence against nurses is becoming more common. One of the legal nurse consultants whom I coach tells me that in her hospital, every single day, a patient assaults a nurse.

Is that what you want for yourself? Is that what you can look forward to if you don't take a risk and consider a new way of using your nursing skills to be compensated for at a higher level?

Perhaps you work on a nursing unit with a manager who is not your favorite person, or you work with a bully in your work environment. And you're tired of watching the tension. You're tired of the stress. You're tired of getting up early in the morning and not seeing your kids until they're getting ready for bed. Or you're tired of being awake all night and then getting off duty and not having time when you're awake while your family is awake.

Or your shifts keep changing. You're going from days to evenings to nights, and you never can catch up with your sleep.

The one thing that I want you to know is that, yes, there are risks when you go into legal nurse consulting. However, there are tremendous rewards. That's key.

Going Deeper
I wrote the first book in my *Creating a Successful LNC Business* series on how to start an LNC business.

In the book, I ask, "Does this sound like you?"

- You want to start or grow your legal nurse consulting business.
- You need a group of raving fans who will recommend you to their attorney colleagues.
- You want to build a strong business that will pay your bills and give you security.

Here's what you gain from *How to Start a Legal Nurse Consulting Business*:

- Understand the fears of attorneys to determine the needs of your ideal client.
- Discover how motivation affects your ability to reach ideal clients.
- Learn how to talk attorneys' language to sell the benefits of working with you.

Throughout this book series, I share specific strategies to use your legal nurse consulting skills to help your clients so that they view you as indispensable.

Order the book here:
http://lnc.tips/creatingseries

See the end of this book for a complete listing of the books in this series.

Chapter 6 Overcoming Risks in Legal Nurse Consulting

I had been reviewing cases as an expert witness for about seven years when I decided that I needed to make more of an effort to meet attorneys in person. I'm a shy person, an introverted person, and it takes a lot of energy for me to be able to walk into a room with a smile plastered on my face and not know a soul. In addition, I am under pressure to make a good impression and meet people who might hire me. That, to me, is not fun. If you're extroverted, you thrive in that environment. If you're introverted, you know exactly what I mean.

The first time I exhibited at an attorney conference, I went to an attorney conference in New Jersey. I was terrified but committed to myself that I would do it again.

The second time I went into a room to meet attorneys was when I walked into the Waldorf Astoria in New York City to meet attorneys attending a national conference. I was scared out of my mind.

I rented table space at the conference and brought my assistant to help me meet and greet attorneys. She was equally shy. Half the time, I wanted to hide behind it. But I had paid a lot of money and put much effort into getting to that beautiful hotel. In addition to the idea of meeting attorneys all day long, the environment intimidated me. There were mirrors and chandeliers and marble floors and velvet curtains. It was an opulent setting.

At my booth, I had a bowl to collect business cards for a drawing. I planned to pick the card of the attorney who looked like the most likely prospect. There was nothing random about my drawing.

I pulled the card of a man who was one of the partners of a law firm with offices in six cities in New Jersey and New York.

Although I did not remember meeting him, I decided he would win the prize. His office was about an hour and a half away from my home, so I called him up to make an appointment to deliver the prize.

I said, "I met you in New York, and you've won a prize at my drawing. I'd like to arrange to deliver it to you." He replied, "You'll have to speak louder. I'm in my private helicopter."

My hand was sweating; I almost hung up. A little voice of self-doubt said, "Pat, who do you think you are? Do you want to deliver a prize to a man who's got a private helicopter? Are you really in that league?" I said to that little voice, "Stop! I'm not giving up that easily."

When I entered his office, we planned to have lunch. Before we could leave to go to the restaurant, he said to me, "I've got this case I want you to look at while you're here. It involves an infant who received an overdose of potassium chloride. He received it by IV push. Can you take a look at this?"

He held up a little black-capped 30 cc multi-dose vial of potassium chloride. I was very familiar with the drug. I said to him, "Nurses are not supposed to give this drug IV push." The defendant nurse was supposed to give three meq and instead gave 30 meq. That overdose put the child into cardiac arrest. Although he was successfully resuscitated, he had anoxic brain damage and quadriparesis.

I told the attorney, "Not only did she give ten times more than she was supposed to, but she should never have given it by IV push."

He said, "Are you sure she shouldn't have given it by IV push?"

"Oh yes, there's a list in every hospital, which states what drugs nurses are allowed to give. And I know that potassium chloride by IV push is not allowed."

"How do you know there's such a list?"

"Because I was responsible for updating that list and teaching nurses about that list in the hospital where I worked."

"I've had six doctors look at this case, and none of them realized that the nurse wasn't supposed to give this drug. How do you know this?"

"Because I'm a nurse."

We never got to lunch that day. After I reviewed the records of the child's case, he handed me a set of records of a man who had a stroke during surgery.

Lunch was a bowl of Japanese seaweed that he'd gotten as takeout. Three hours later, I left the law firm with a new client and two cases.

Eventually, after much resistance, the defense attorney handed over the list of medications nurses were permitted to give by IV push at that hospital. The list confirmed that the neonatal nurse was not allowed to give potassium chloride IV push. My client settled that case for $7 million.

After that first office visit, he started working with me closely. This attorney gave me so much business that he put my oldest son through four years of an Ivy League college education.

I'm working with him today. He returned to me as a client in February 2021 and said, "Pat, I've got a case I want you to help me with."

I replied, "I had a five-year non-compete agreement with the woman who bought my business. It's been six years since I sold the company. Tell me about your case." We've been working on cases ever since.

About three years after I first started working with this attorney, I said to him, "I've seen your Porsche. I've seen your BMW. But where's your private helicopter? Where do you keep that?"

He looked at me and said, "Private helicopter? What are you talking about?"

I said, "When I called you to make this appointment, you said you were in your private helicopter. And that's why it was so noisy."

He said, "Pat, I was probably standing under a fan in the men's room."

I thought, "What if I had hung up on him? What if I had listened to that little voice of doubt that said, 'Pat, you're not in the right league to deal with this man?'" That little voice can shoot down your dreams before you have a chance to fulfill them.

Chapter 7 What Does it Take to Get Started?

The primary step in getting started is to look at your value as a nurse. Put aside all the thoughts about, "I don't know the law," or "I don't know what the legal terms mean," and ask yourself:

- What are your key strengths?
- What do you love to do?
- Are you equipped to do this type of role?
- Do you like digging into medical records?
- Are you fascinated by details?
- Do you enjoy writing reports?
- Do you enjoy researching and learning?
- Do you like to teach?

If you can answer yes to those questions, you have the qualities that help attorneys handle their cases. Those are the individuals who succeed in this field.

By the time I sold my independent LNC business in 2015, I had 200 nurses, doctors, and other healthcare providers under contract to review cases for my company. I taught them how to be expert witnesses and subcontractors, review cases, write reports, respond to clients, and testify effectively. In many situations, I gave them their first case and helped them launch their expert witness or LNC career.

The people who have those qualities that I just listed on the previous page are the ones who are successful.

First, look at your talents and your strengths. Are you cut out for this work? Not everyone is. Not every nurse has writing skills. It may surprise you that not every nurse is detail-oriented because when nurses take care of patients, we have to be incredibly attentive to details. If you give 500 milligrams instead of 50 milligrams of a drug, you could end up injuring the patient.

Next, you need to ask yourself why you want this role. What fascinates you about working with the law and legal cases? What do you find so appealing?

You might have heard in your LNC program that this was a quick get rich profession. You're going to get business right away. Attorneys will be falling all over themselves to hire you.

If you heard this, you've been misled.

You need encouragement to start a business and to be successful in a business. Success does not happen overnight. It takes determination, business knowledge, and support.

Some nurses are in the right place at the right time to make a connection or to get an introduction to an attorney, and their businesses take off. But for most people, this is a slow process that requires determination, taking action, and not giving up.

Tell yourself, "I'm in this for the long haul. I could be so close to success and getting my first case. But if you give up before you get there, you will be kicking yourself and saying, "I wasted time, I wasted money. Even though I went through an educational program, I didn't get cases right away." You could be giving up when the first case is right around the corner.

Chapter 8 Paths to Getting Cases

In the first and second editions of *Paths to Legal Nurse Consulting*, I shared stories of how some of my LNC colleagues got into the field.

Some nurses got their first cases from friends, family members, acquaintances, or random strangers. A few were approached out of the blue, and others applied for in-house jobs. Many persisted in the face of rejection. For some LNCs who worked in risk management or quality assurance, getting the first case was a byproduct of their role.

I've excerpted some of their stories here and organized them into a few categories. You'll see there is no one uniform way of getting started.

Family, Friends, and Acquaintances

It took me ten months to get my first case; I think my husband was starting to question the significant expenses I incurred. Once one decides to become a legal nurse consultant, the biggest hurdle seems to be

marketing and how to get clients. At every opportunity, I told people about my new business. My first client was an attorney whose son played sports with my son. I reviewed a personal injury case for him.
Connie Paine

My husband moved from a defense firm where he did insurance law to his own two-person firm where he practiced real estate law, and his law partner specialized in personal injury cases. Occasionally, they asked me to look at the medical records of a personal injury case that they were thinking of taking or had taken. They wanted to know what injuries their client or potential client had sustained. At the time, I had no idea that nurses were doing this kind of work and getting paid for it.
Marjorie Pugatch

My career began in 1998 when a couple in our church was arrested for starving their 15-year-old disabled daughter to death. I offered to analyze the girl's medical and school records pro bono. My goal was to find the truth.

I used an excellent resource, Pat Iyer's, *Principles and Practice of Legal Nurse Consulting, Second Edition.* I spent two

years working with criminal defense attorneys, analyzing records, and research. I testified as a fact witness in two trials.
Lisa Kuipers

In 1996, my oldest daughter went to law school intending to protect the rights of the elderly. In her senior year, she did an internship with a New York law firm specializing in medical malpractice and was assigned a case to review. The firm instructed her to use any available sources to develop her case.

We were on the phone until 2 AM the night before her assignment was due! She was terrified after speaking with her friends as she discovered she was the only one who concluded that there was no physician liability since the patient did not follow the doctor's orders. The professor, a partner in the law firm, successfully represented that client. However, he agreed with her conclusion and offered her an associate position in his firm after graduation.

As fate would have it, I was in the process of a Joint Commission survey in one of my facilities when I received my LNC certification. The Joint Commission nurse I was working with overheard me speaking

with my administrator about my LNC certification and suggested that I call a friend of hers in Florida who worked for a law firm and was looking for legal nurse consultants. Ever since then, I have never been without legal nurse consulting opportunities.
Georgette Bieber

In 1986, while I held a dual position of Certified Nurse Midwife and hospital administrator in the OB-GYN department at a major teaching hospital, a colleague approached me to review a medical malpractice case involving a midwife. I remember being surprised that she would ask me, primarily because I had no clue about what I was supposed to do and had no knowledge of the role and function of an LNC. I was concerned about being qualified to meet the attorney's needs due to my inexperience in the field.

Ultimately, I contacted the attorney, who was based in Florida and represented the plaintiff. At that point, I embarked on a journey that would change my life.
Shirley White-Walker

Early in 2007, I was dating a lawyer (he did not work in malpractice or PI) whose niece was in a car accident. She had a poor medical outcome and high medical bills. I reviewed her chart and bills and found the information the attorney needed to get the bills reduced or written off. They were not interested in a suit, just parity for the outcomes.

The economy was beginning to crash, and those thousands of dollars I was going to make in recruiting had added up to zero at this point, so at his suggestion, I began marketing to attorneys for medical malpractice work.
Suzanne Rector

In my childhood, I always wanted to be Perry Mason. While I was home having babies, I received a brochure for a seminar on legal nurse consulting. Later, I realized that I was interested in the law but did not want to be a lawyer.

When I saw this brochure, I wondered if this could be a niche for me. I called five lawyers I knew to ask if they had ever heard of legal nurse consulting and if they thought there was a need for this kind of work. I received two cases from five calls, and I was in business (how I wish it were that easy now).
Mindy Cohen

While waiting to catch a flight at the Richmond International Airport, I started a conversation with a fellow passenger. We discovered we were both nurses. Diana was working as a nurse paralegal at a local defense firm. She was happy to learn that I worked full-time in a PACU at a tertiary teaching hospital. She asked if I had ever done any expert witness work. I had no idea what she meant.

Diana explained the role briefly to me as she gave me her business card. "Send me your resume when you get back," she said. "We're always looking for nurses to review cases." I stuck the card in my purse. I spent a few hours polishing the document and sent it to Diana. She promptly thanked me and said she would keep me in mind for future cases. Six months went by, and I had heard nothing. Then the phone rang. It was Diana, and she had a case she wanted me to consider reviewing. I agreed.
Dana Jolly

Advertisements for Inhouse Jobs

While I was working in a large teaching hospital, a colleague left our ICU to work in the hospital's "in-house" legal department. When I spoke to her about her job, it sounded intriguing, and I began looking for similar opportunities. Early in my nursing career, I was interested in process improvement and assisted with several quality assurance projects on my unit.

One day while reading the newspaper, I located a blind ad for a legal nurse consultant. I sent my CV and was called for a telephone interview within a few days, followed by an in-person interview the following day.

The attorney, who specialized in plaintiff personal injury, explained that part of the interview process was to take a case home that evening and have it completed by the next day. Not knowing better, I complied with his request, despite having minimal legal knowledge and no training or experience as an LNC. The next day, I returned with my work product, and he hired me for the position.
Alexa Schneider

Shortly after we moved to the suburbs of Detroit, I was offered a position in a cardiac step-down unit, but something made me tell the recruiter that I wanted to look at the other hospitals in the area before committing to the position. That night I read

the want ads and saw a job advertised by a nearby law firm for a "nurse paralegal" The ad read, "***Wanted: RN with strong medical background; we will teach you the legal.***" I told my husband the position had my name on it. I applied; I interviewed; I was hired. And so, in October 1987, I apprehensively started my new career as a "nurse paralegal."
Marty Morris

My career as a legal nurse consultant began in the 1980s when I answered a newspaper advertisement for a position as a nurse paralegal at a defense firm. I had no legal experience or legal education but, undaunted, I applied for the job.

The interviewer told me I would not have to perform a paralegal's typical duties and needed no paralegal background. The law firm wanted a nurse to review medical records and prepare reports for The Joint Medical Defense, a consortium of attorney defendants handling asbestos cases. Recognizing that an experienced nurse can perform medical records reviews with more efficiency and thoroughness than attorneys, the attorney hired me.
Jane Barone

On the way back to graduate school for a Ph.D. in nursing, I answered a want ad in January 1986 that asked for a nurse to review obstetric records for a plaintiff attorney; his practice was 80% birth injury. After reviewing two cases as part of the interview/selection process, I told him, "I am the most qualified person for this job, and if I don't get it, I want to know the reason why." A year later, he told me that was why he hired me; he wanted to work with anyone who could say that to him.
Diane Ellenberger

Getting LNC Work From a Position

My hospital background was primarily in the med-surg ICU of a regional trauma hospital. In 1985, I became the nurse manager of a forensic psychological practice. These patients were referred by treating physicians, nurse case managers, employers, and both plaintiff and defense attorneys.

I had never heard of a "legal nurse consultant," but I knew that specialists needed information about the care rendered by other physicians. I developed a medical chronology as part of every psychological evaluation; this offered a "picture" of the patient as a person rather than a body part. These chronologies helped both the attorneys and the treating physicians since years of care would be summarized in just a few pages. I have now analyzed over 6,000 workers' compensation cases.

I first heard the term "legal nurse consultant" in 2005 and was immediately drawn to the concept of forming an independent identity. Years of hospital work, attorney interface, writing record summaries, and dealing with medical experts laid the foundation for this career.
Alice Adams

Since my first few years working in malpractice claims management, I had begun to think about starting a legal nurse consulting business. My husband was an entrepreneur and gave me the "start a business" bug. In my two-income family, I had always had "the stable job and good insurance."

After having my first child, I enjoyed the generous option of working from home a few days a week in my work as a malpractice claims manager. But change was underway in my organization. My bosses' boss was getting a new boss. My comfortable position working from home was no longer going to be available. I decided it was time to give launching an LNC business some serious consideration.

While continuing my full-time work as a malpractice claims manager, I had the opportunity to review a couple of medical malpractice cases for a local defense attorney with whom I was associated through my company.
Laura Averette

My journey harkens back to a day in 1979 when I became disillusioned with the nursing profession. I went so far as to tear up my license, swearing never again to practice nursing. Next, I worked for an information technology business as an office manager, only to be frustrated and unfulfilled. What was I going to do with the rest of my working years? I was not one to sit and do nothing, and I have always enjoyed a challenge.

As luck would have it, a temporary service telephoned and asked me if I would be interested in a case management position with a national managed care company. Despite my lack of case management experience, the employer concluded I had

the skills for the job. One of the best pieces of advice I received was, "Keep your mouth shut, listen and follow directions." I took the advice, went to work as a case manager, and was promoted to supervisor of the insurance carrier's corporate accounts. I had found my next nursing challenge.
Barbara King

After completing my bachelor's degree, I was promoted to manager of case management, physician audit, medical review, and the pre-certification sections. This position provided a new way to use my nursing knowledge and experience that I enjoyed. During my employment with the health insurance company, I assisted the corporate attorneys with several legal cases. My first case involved investigating possible fraud by an ambulance company. After finding ample evidence of fraud, the insurance company filed suit against the ambulance company. I served as the expert witness in this federal case. My legal nurse consulting career had begun, although I did not know it at the time; I loved working fraud cases. After the successful litigation of this fraud case, I was asked to assist the legal department in several other matters.
Kathy Ferrell

One day, I came across a beautiful brochure from a legal nurse consulting company and was intrigued by this entirely new aspect of nursing. I first learned of legal nurse consulting when I was quality manager for a supplemental staffing agency.

I had the opportunity to work very closely with a registered nurse who was also the agency's attorney. I was fascinated and in awe of this woman who seemed to really have her pulse on how to ensure safe practice. It wasn't easy managing nurses who were p.r.n. employees. It was a potentially huge liability for the facility that agreed to hire the nurse, and for our organization if we sent someone who was not professional or well trained. It was a big job, and my position was instrumental in ensuring safe care.

Once, I participated in a deposition at the corporate office, since the complaint came through my office from the facility. It was a wrongful death case. When I saw the wonderfully constructed brochure about legal nurse consulting more than five years later, I realized that I had already done some of that work in my deposition.
Rhonda Haney

Random Calls from Strangers

The opportunity to explore legal nurse consulting as a career came through a phone call from a legal assistant asking if I would be available to review a case for standards of care in a labor and delivery setting. A colleague had given her my contact information. Intrigued, I said yes. Several days later, I received my first case.
Brenda Murphy

In the summer of 2006, an attorney in Raleigh called and asked me to review a case from 1983. At this point, I was not aware of what a legal nurse consultant was, but I agreed; that is how I started my legal consulting career.

The following month I received another call from an attorney in South Carolina asking me to review a shoulder dystocia case. I was thrilled but did not know what to charge. When he asked me about a retainer, I didn't know what to say, so I said "sure." I blurted out, " $500," and he said, "No problem." The next day I had the records and the retainer.
Janis Cox

I was working in my office at Jersey City Medical Center in 1991 as Director of Nursing when a call came in. The person on the other end said, "I am an attorney in Washington DC…" and told me about his predicament, which was that he needed someone, a nurse, to review medical records.

He asked, or rather pleaded with me to meet him at my convenience, any place I wanted, and for me to help him. I said, "OK…how about the Holiday Inn lobby in Springfield, NJ, on X date and time?" I didn't ask any of the usual or obvious pertinent questions such as, "What is this all about?" or "How did you find me?" or "What am I supposed to do?"

As I approached the hotel, I abruptly thought, "What if he is a murderer or something? What am I doing? Oh well, it's a public place. What can happen?"
Kathy Martin

Networking

Networking has always served me well in my nursing career and has also helped me grow as a legal nurse consultant. Information on the AALNC website directed me to our New Jersey chapter, with which I have been actively involved since 2005.

While the dinners at The Rutgers Club are always a pleasurable culinary adventure, and the speakers over the years have added to my knowledge base, the best thing about our chapter meetings is the ability to network with fellow LNCs. We have been able to share personal triumphs and commiserate over that attorney who raked us over the coals. Best of all, it opened the door of subcontracting for me.

As an active member of NJ AALNC, I was able to work on my first case as a subcontractor under a very experienced (and very patient) LNC. Mrs. D's report traveled back and forth through cyberspace until it had fulfilled all the attorney's requirements. By the time I had produced the final work product, I felt I had given birth to my fourth child. My mentor's patience was never-ending, and although she may have mumbled under her breath, she never let her frustration show. She respected my nursing knowledge while assisting me to look at things from a legal perspective. I will be forever grateful. Subsequent employers

were not always as nurturing, but I continued to learn and grow.
Louanne Nicotra

I met a couple of nurses who had been doing consulting work with workers' compensation attorneys for over ten years. Eager to learn and ready to start my new career, I asked them if I could intern with them. But they were swamped and suggested I do some work in nurse case management or life care planning. I continued to market to attorneys and do my clinical work.

About a year after taking my LNC course, I eventually got a call from one of the nurses I had asked about interning. She wanted to know if I was still interested in working as a nurse consultant. She knew of an attorney who did workers' compensation cases who had recently opened her law firm and wanted a nurse to do some timelines.

She introduced us, and I began work immediately and continued to do so for about 2twoyears. I did chronologies of the medical records for all of her cases and helped with case development. I went to regular appointments and independent

medical exams (IME) with the claimant and reported back to the attorney.
Teri Levin

Going Deeper
To get the full understanding of how each of the 42 authors entered the LNC field and how they developed their businesses, order the ***Path to Legal Nurse Consulting, Second Edition*** at http://LNC.tips/path

Chapter 9 How One Client Became Many

As I shared earlier, when I first started reviewing cases as an expert, I sent letters to 20 attorneys. In addition to the shattered IV bottle case, I got a call from another attorney whose case went to trial a few months later with me as the defense expert. Eventually, I got calls from all of the attorneys to whom I sent letters.

Peter, the attorney who gave me my first case, liked working with me, and so I took another risk. I said to him, "I'm interested in starting to work with attorneys. Would you be willing is to give me the names of ten attorneys who you think would be amenable to me contacting them and asking them if I can assist them with their cases?"

That was a bold request. Most people, when they ask for introductions, request the names of one or two people. Not knowing any better, I asked him for ten, and he sat down and wrote them for me.

I contacted all ten attorneys, and eventually, I got cases from all of them. They included both plaintiff and defense lawyers.

I learned that by taking the risk of asking for attorneys' names, I got results. But what if I hadn't asked? What if I had just waited for people to find me? I started building up my expert witness work in 1988 when people didn't have websites. I got my first site in 1995 and was one of the first people in the LNC field to have a website.

It was because I acted, because I stuck my neck out, that I got results. I didn't wait for people to find me. I went looking for them. Then I showed them through my knowledge and capabilities that I could assist them. I asked for feedback. "How did I do? Is there anything that I could have done differently?" I went through many depositions and trials as an expert witness and testified in sometimes grueling circumstances.

I asked my clients, "Tell me how I did. Do I need to change anything? What do you think was strong? What do I need to work on?" They gave me answers. But if I hadn't asked them, they wouldn't necessarily have given me that feedback. I was always willing to learn, always seeking out more information, and figuring out how I could help my clients by improving my skills.

After reviewing medical-surgical cases for two years, I got a call from a plaintiff attorney handling an emergency department case. He asked me to be the expert. I declined and referred him to a colleague who was a well-credentialed emergency department nursing clinical specialist. She took the case.

"I wonder if there is a business supplying expert witnesses?" I thought. Spurred on by that question, I created a framework for finding, training, referring, and supervising expert witnesses. The first expert I hired was that emergency department clinical specialist.

My company billed for the experts, which resulted in a lucrative and ultimately saleable multi-million-dollar company.

Going Deeper

- Would you like to increase your client base and get more cases from existing clients?
- Would you like to know proven strategies that exponentially increase your success as a legal nurse consultant?

- Would it be helpful to find the types of offline and online venues that are great opportunities for you to meet attorneys?
- Would you be interested in knowing what blocks you have that might be sabotaging your networking efforts?

In my book, *Networking for LNCs*, I provide a step-by-step process for asking for introductions. When you read this book, you will

- Address your objections to networking, get ready for the hunt, and discover how to research local networking opportunities.
- Develop the success mindset needed to effectively connect with people who are either attorneys or those who can introduce you to attorneys.
- Gain a step-by-step process for asking for referrals and follow up with opportunities.

Get your copy here:
http://LNC.tips/networkingbook.

Chapter 10 No Regrets

What will life look like if you don't persist in getting your first LNC case? Imagine you've gone through your legal nurse consulting program. You're held back. You've got people in your ear saying, "You can't start a business." Or nurses you work with say, "Do you really want to work with attorneys?"

You hesitate. You say, "I think a good time to start my business would be at the beginning of the year." Now it's June. Are you going to wait six months? Are you going to hesitate? Are you going to lose your momentum?

Some of the LNCs who come to me for coaching to help them with their LNC business reveal their timeline of going months or years without their first case.

In the future, are you going to say, "I'm getting older. I'm getting tired," or "I'm fearful of failing. Now isn't the right time to start a business. My mother is sick. I need to pay attention to her." Or "I'm too uneducated. I don't have a master's degree like you do, Pat."

You've got a dozen excuses. One nurse told me that the only legal nurse consultants who were successful in getting started were dating or married to attorneys.

As one of the LNCs who served as president of our national organization, the American Association of Legal Nurse Consultants, I met hundreds of LNCs. As I listened to her talk, I thought, "I only know two legal nurse consultants who are married to attorneys."

You can always come up with excuses. If you don't take the step to start your business, will you wake up one day and say, "My back is injured; I can't get out of bed today. I'm getting burned out, and I'm too tired to continue this kind of work."

Or you could get laid off. Hospitals and healthcare systems merge, and you might be made redundant.

Or you might be in a situation where your unit or your clinical is short-staffed, which is increasingly a problem in today's COVID era. Nurses are leaving and getting jobs at travel agencies and getting paid significantly more than they get paid when they work on staff in a hospital, for example.

And you're short-staffed, and you're working harder and harder and harder in an environment that's very stressful.

You'll be sitting there saying, "I should have started my business. I wouldn't have to be going through this."

I recommend that you keep your job. You say, "What? Pat, you just listed all the negatives." Here's what I mean. "Don't quit your day job" has significant meaning in this field. Many LNCs build their businesses on the side until it's generating a steady flow of work and solid cash flow. And then you can pull your foot away step by step from a full-time job to a part-time job.

However, if you don't take that first step, if you don't put your foot out, if you don't take risks, you will never get to the point where you have the satisfaction of owning your own business and not being dependent on an employer for a paycheck.

Chapter 11 The First Step

The first step towards getting your first case is to look at your goals. What do you want to accomplish in your life and your business?

Many people use the SMART goals model for defining goals. SMART stands for Specific, Measurable, Attainable, Realistic, and Trackable. Think of them as you would the patient outcomes we include in a nursing care plan.

- When do you want to start marketing your business?
- When do you want to start getting cases?
- When will you open up your shop to accept business from attorneys?
- How are you going to gain clients?
- What number of clients make sense for you?

Knowing your SMART goals requires you to take action.

Procrastination is our version of a dream stealer. If you find yourself hesitating, ask yourself:

- What will I gain personally and financially by completing this task?
- What losses will I suffer if I do not complete this task?
- Have I ever tried to accomplish a job like this before?
- What was the outcome of my last attempt?
- How did that make me feel? (Emotionally, physically, and mentally)?
- Who fed into those feelings of success or failure?

My colleague Kathleen Aston developed this procrastination contract, which I modified.

Contract for Procrastination Planning

How do I feel when I complete a task or goal about which I have been procrastinating?

Emotionally:

Physically:

What happens to me when I think about what I have put off and have not yet accomplished?

Emotionally:

Physically:

What is the most critical thing I need to do right now to increase the revenues of my business?

What do I need to help me complete this task? (Consider people, technology, training.) TIME is not an acceptable answer.

Find the time in your calendar by canceling anything that is not revenue-generating until you accomplish this task or goal.

When will I work on this task?

How will I feel when I complete this task? How will completing this task improve my business, my life, and that of those around me? How will I feel about myself?

I hope you have had a few "ah-has" through completing the worksheet above. Now, I want you to focus on HOW GOOD it felt when you accomplished a task in the past. Repeat this process worksheet for the TOP three tasks or goals you need to accomplish but have been putting off. Tape them up above your desk.

Wrap-Up! Here's the fun part. What satisfying reward will I plan for myself to enjoy once I have accomplished this task and/or goal?

Return to this worksheet in six months on _____(date)

SIX MONTHS CHECK UP:

What have the benefits been to your business and your personal sense of accomplishment and worth by having decided to complete this task six months ago?

Aha!

What did completing this task teach you about procrastination and why you put this task off for so long in the first place? What was really stopping you?

You may never totally conquer your fears, perfectionism, or procrastination, but you can tackle them one by one. Think about the positive impact your business can create for you.

Examine your degree of confidence. If you sit there saying, "Maybe nobody will want to hire me, maybe I'm not going to be good at this job," you are talking yourself out of taking a risk.

One of my *Legal Nurse Podcast* guests, Amy Puls, is a nurse practitioner whose full-time clinical practice disappeared in 2020 when her office shut down during the pandemic. She replaced her full-time NP role with a part-time NP role and part-time LNC role. Reflect on what Amy had to say about making mistakes:

> That first (medical malpractice) case was interesting because I hadn't read medical charts from that standpoint. As nurses, we read medical charts all the time, but I learned that to read it from the viewpoint of a legal nurse consultant or an expert witness, you have to have a very unbiased opinion, and you have to see it from

both sides, whether you're working for the defense or the plaintiff.

For instance, if you're working for the defense, you have to also read it from a plaintiff's viewpoint because the defense attorney is hiring you as the expert. They don't want to have unexpected topics that come up from the plaintiff that you, as the expert, maybe didn't see and didn't share with them.

As the expert, you will prepare them from both sides and give them your expert opinion on how the defense will prevail in that case. That was eye-opening for me, honestly. And I didn't do that at first, and I did make many mistakes.

And the attorney was very patient with me, but he was also very honest. He put me in my place, which was good. And if he hadn't done that, I wouldn't have learned that you do have to go into it with an open mind and look at it from both sides. Whether you agree with their part of the case or not, you have to tell them why you disagree or why you agree, and what potentially could happen from the opposing counsel or the opposing expert, what they could bring up.

Amy continued to market and got more cases. But what if she had her confidence so soundly shaken that she wasn't willing to try again?

Tell yourself when you stand in front of your mirror, "I am a successful legal nurse consultant. I am capable of doing this work and helping attorneys. I will make a positive difference in my attorneys' clients' lives and in the lives of their clients."

Affirmations are a valuable technique. People put affirmations on the refrigerator, on their car dashboard, on their mirror in their bathroom. When you repeat affirmations, you are conditioning your mind for success.

Repeating your affirmations ingrains them into your mind and your unconscious. After a while, the new thought pattern takes over for the old thought pattern.

Say your affirmations aloud in the car. These concepts become your new thoughts; they become your new defaults.

And don't listen to negative people. Shut them out. I know it's hard to shut family members out who are negative. I get that. But if you have negative friends, colleagues, and relatives trying to undercut your dream, you can label them as dream stealers. Say, "I'm not going to listen to the dream stealers."

"I'm going to pursue my goal of starting my business. I'm going to reach out to attorneys. I'm going to demonstrate my expertise. I will use language that shows I understand their pressures and their needs. I'm going to craft my marketing messages so that I'm speaking directly to what they are looking for, what will make their lives easier so they can practice law more effectively."

Keeping a journal of your efforts is helpful. Documenting what you're doing each day to help establish your business will show how far you have progressed. One simple step each day will accumulate into massive action and put you ahead of the other legal nurse consultants who have gone through a program and sit back and wait for attorneys to find them. And the attorneys are not going to find them.

Put yourself forward by using networking for visibility. Examine your mindset, your beliefs about your successes and capabilities.

Tackle the issues that cause you to procrastinate. Set achievable goals and use affirmations to influence your mindset. Strive for a positive way of looking at the world and avoid negative thinking and people.

The entrepreneurial spirit is a special one. Treasure the fact that you have the courage to set your course as you embrace the challenges of this exciting field of nursing. Consider and positively manage how your mindset affects the way you tackle the challenges of starting and running a business.

If you've never had a case, it's easy to say, "This is too complicated for me," or "there's too much to learn," or "it's overwhelming." But if you stay in that mindset, you will never break free from where you are. And you'll never experience the successes that come along with being a legal nurse consultant.

Going Deeper
Get Amy's full podcast at podcast.legalnursebusiness.com. It is #472. She has excellent tips about using LinkedIn to get clients.

How to Analyze Medical Records is my most popular book. I consider this one of the essential books for a new LNC.

Order it at this link: http://LNC.tips/creatingseries.

Chapter 12 Getting Help

One of the principles that I found in building my own business and being successful in this field is that this is not a business where you can be a loner and expect to succeed.

You need to be surrounded by other people who understand the way you think, who cheer you on, encouraging you to persist in the face of discouragement or very slow responses.

I work with legal nurse consultants, both individually and in group programs. My group program is called **LNC Success Connection.** It consists of education support, accountability, and access to me to ask questions. I periodically open the program to new members and maintain a waitlist between those admission times.

I also work one-on-one with individuals looking for a higher level of interaction or more personal experiences with me, as opposed to a group setting. This **Flex Coaching** is also available when the LNC Success Connection is closed to new members.

I've designed both types of coaching to move you forward. I'll share the lessons I learned that I don't want you to learn the hard way,

I will show you what you need to know to build a successful business.

You can learn these techniques by trial and error. But you will shortcut your learning by working with me as a business coach to help you start and grow your business.

If you want to use your nursing, education, and communication skills, and your ability to be focused on small details in a new way, legal nurse consulting can provide you with a satisfying and lucrative career.

Only about 10% of the world is wired to be entrepreneurs. We find each other we recognize each other.

We don't want to be employees for the rest of our lives. Maybe it's okay part-time. Perhaps it's okay on an occasional basis. But you want to be in charge of your destiny. And unless you grab the opportunities associated with starting a business, you are at risk of feeling unhappy and dissatisfied.

Take a step forward. Considering all of the factors that go into starting a business may be daunting. However, being an entrepreneur can be intensely rewarding. You're helping attorneys help their clients, whether defense or plaintiff. You're using your nursing skills in a way that compensates you well.

As an LNC, you are setting yourself up for successes and grateful clients in a field where your knowledge is essential for attorneys handling medical cases. Don't be stuck and dissatisfied with your current life. There's something in you that got attracted to legal nurse consulting.

I say reach for that brass ring. Take risks. Step out, go for your dream. Achieve your goals and reach for the greater freedom and flexibility that comes along with owning a business.

Going Deeper
Contact me to explore options for getting coaching and support. Reach me through my email at patiyer@legalnursebusiness.com. And

check out the options on this page:
http://LNC.tips/VIPC.

Other Books by Pat Iyer

Creating A Successful Legal Nurse Consulting Practice Series, published by The Pat Iyer Group:

How to Heat a Fiery Brand for Your LNC business: Tips to Be Noticeable (Book 14)

Your Ideal Attorney Clients: How to Connect With Them by Speaking Their Language (Book 13)

21 Tips to Run Your LNC Business Efficiently: How to Excel (Book 12)

Networking for LNCs (Book 11)

How to Create Lasting Attorney-LNC Relationships (Book 10)

How to be a Successful LNC: Tips for Your Business (Book 9)

How to Manage Your LNC Business: Top Tips for Success (Book 8)

How to Grow Your LNC Business: Secrets of Success (Book 7)

How to Get More Cases: Marketing Secrets for LNCs (Book 6)

How to Get More Clients: Sales Secrets for LNCs (Book 5)

How to be a Successful Expert Witness (Book 4)

How to Analyze Medical Records: A Primer for LNCs (Book 3)

Legal Nurse Consultant Marketing (Book 2)

How to Start a Legal Nurse Consulting Practice (Book 1)

Additional books by Pat Iyer as Author, Editor, Coeditor, or Coauthor

Powerful Storytelling in Business: How to Captivate Your Clients (Book 5)

Why Become a Better Writer: How Writing Skills Help You Thrive (Book 4)

How to Overcome Writing Barriers: Wipe Out What Blocks You (Book 3)

52 Writing Tips: Fast and Easy Ways to Polish Your Writing (Book 2)

Path to Legal Nurse Consulting: Collective Wisdom of Successful LNCs, Second Edition (Book 1)

Analyzing Emergency Department Medical Malpractice Cases, The Pat Iyer Group

Analyzing Falls, Pressure Sores and IV Therapy Cases, The Pat Iyer Group

Honing Your Legal Nurse Consulting Practice, The Pat Iyer Group

Building Blocks of a Legal Nurse Consulting Business, The Pat Iyer Group

Secrets of Growing Your Legal Nurse Consulting Business, The Pat Iyer Group

Iyer, P. and Brown, Al S., **How to Get Published**, The Pat Iyer Group

Safeguard your Ambulatory Care Nursing Practice, The Pat Iyer Group

Social Media Marketing for Legal Professionals, The Pat Iyer Group

Iyer, P., Levin, B., Ashton, K. and Powell, V. (Editors), **Nursing Malpractice, Fourth Edition,** Lawyers and Judges Publishing Company

Iyer, P. and Levin, B. (Editors), **Medical-Legal Aspects of Medical Records, Second Edition,** Lawyers and Judges Publishing Company

Legal Nurse Consultants' Handbook, The Pat Iyer Group

Gray-Micelli, D., Capezuti, E., Lawson, W. and Iyer, P., **Falls Handbook: From Public to Patient Settings: Clinical and Medical-Legal Perspectives of Falls Across the Lifespan,** The Pat Iyer Group

Iyer, P. (Editor), **Nursing Home Litigation: Investigation and Case Preparation, Second Edition,** Lawyers and Judges Publishing Company

Iyer, P., Aken, J. and Condon, K. (Editors), **Business Principles of Legal Nurse Consulting,** Francis and Taylor

Iyer, P. and Camp, N., **Nursing Documentation: A Nursing Process Approach, Fourth Edition,** The Pat Iyer Group

Iyer. P. (Editor), **Medical-Legal Aspects of Pain and Suffering,** Tucson, AZ, Lawyers and Judges Publishing Company

Iyer, P. (Editor), **Principles and Practices of Legal Nurse Consulting, Second Edition,** Francis and Taylor

Barbacci, M., Browsky, D., Calderone, A., Cantwell-Davis, S., Clark, K., Iyer, P., **Essentials of Medical Record Analysis,** AALNC

Iyer, P., Taptich, B. and Bernocchi-Losey, D., **Nursing Process and Nursing Diagnosis,** Third Edition, WB Saunders

Taptich, B., Iyer, P. and Bernocchi-Losey, D., **Nursing Diagnosis and Care Planning, Second Edition,** WB Saunders

Rowland, L. and Iyer, P. (Editor), **Patient Outcomes in Maternal Child Nursing,** Springhouse

Camp, N. and Iyer, P. (Editor), **Patient Outcomes in Medical-Surgical Nursing,** Springhouse

Whitis, G. and Iyer, P. (Editor), **Patient Outcomes in Pediatric Nursing,** Springhouse

Please Write a Review

When you enjoy a book, it is a natural desire to tell others about it. Most sales platforms provide a way to share your thoughts with a review if you have an account or buy the book. I invite you to write a book review. It is easy. Here are tips that should help, although each platform's process may be a bit different:

On the platform's home page, type the book title or Pat Iyer in the search bar. That should bring you to the page that displays this book.

Scroll down until you see a bar that says, "Write a customer review."

Assign several stars to the book - that match your opinion of the book.

Create a title for the review. This can be a simple phrase, like "Awesome Book." If you are not sure what to say, look at the titles of other book reviews.

It is easiest to write the book in a word processor and then paste it into the review text box on the platform. Your word processor will pick up typos before your review goes public.

Write the review as if you were talking to another person – you are – a person who comes to the platform is has read this book.

Include a description of what you found most helpful. Was it an idea, chapter, tip? Share that with the readers.

Next, you may want to write who you think would most benefit from this book. Is it for beginner LNCs? Or is it more appropriate for LNCs with experience with this topic?

What if you have something negative to say about the book? You may always reach me at patiyer@legalnursebusiness.com to suggest changes in the book.

If you include negative feedback in the review, keep a positive perspective rather than attack the author.

Here are some sample phrases:

While overall the book was good, I would change it by. . .

I don't think this book is right for. . .

I would improve this book by. . .

Before you hit save, read everything over one more time. Authors and readers appreciate book reviews, and they get easier to write with time.

Also, please email me at pat@patiyer.com when you have posted your review.

Thank you,

Pat Iyer

About the Author

Patricia W. Iyer, MSN RN LNCC
President, The Pat Iyer Group
Fort Myers, FL
www.legalnursebusiness.com

Pat discovered legal nurse consulting in 1989 when she attended her first AALNC conference. At that time, nurses who worked with attorneys were called medical-legal consultants. The role and language of this field evolved over the 30+ years Pat grew her independent legal nurse consultant business.

About five years after she started her LNC business, Pat recognized the power of networking at attorney conferences and built her business through the relationships she established.

Starting with her first desk (a board over the top of two 2-drawer filing cabinets), Pat created sales of a million dollars or more per year for the last five years she owned her business.

With an eye towards the eventual sale of her LNC company, Pat started The Pat Iyer Group in 2008 to provide education, coaching, and inspiration to legal nurse consultants. Her many courses, online trainings, and books are located on legalnursebusiness.com.

Currently, Pat works with attorneys as an LNC and coaches legal nurse consultants through her program LNC Success Connection. Get the details at http://LNC.tips/connection. For one-on-one coaching, see http://LNC.tips/VIPC.

Reach Pat through her website, LegalNurseBusiness.com, her email patiyer@legalnursebusiness.com or call 908-391-7933.

Connect with Pat Iyer:

LinkedIn.com/in/patiyer

Facebook.com/patiyer

Twitter.com/patiyer

Websites:

Legalnursebusiness.com

LNCEU.com

Patiyer.com

Watch our videos:
http://LNC.tips/PatiyerYouTube

www.ingramcontent.com/pod-product-compliance
Lightning Source LLC
Chambersburg PA
CBHW051540240526
45465CB00028B/1626